Art in Pompeii and Herculaneum

Paul Roberts with Vanessa Baldwin

THE BRITISH MUSEUM PRESS

First published in 2013 by The British Museum Press
A division of The British Museum Company Ltd
38 Russell Square, London WC1B 3QQ
britishmuseum.org/publishing

A catalogue record for this book is available from the British Library
ISBN: 978-0-7141-2283-0

Designed by Raymonde Watkins
Printed in China by C&C Offset Printing Co., Ltd

The papers used by the British Museum Press are recyclable products
and the manufacturing processes are expected to conform to the
environmental regulations of the country of origin.

FRONT COVER Fresco showing a woman's face. Herculaneum.
H. 19.7 cm, W. 15.4 cm. Naples, MANN 9094

BACK COVER Fresco showing Flora, goddess of flowers and Spring.
Stabiae, Villa of Ariadne. H. 39.5 cm, W. 32.5 cm. Naples,
MANN 8834

FRONT FLAP Mosaic showing a dog. Pompeii, House of Orpheus
(VI,14,20). H. 80 cm, W. 80 cm. Naples, MANN 110666

BACK FLAP Mosaic showing a skeleton holding two wine jugs. Pompeii
(VI, Ins. Occ.19–26). H. 91 cm, W. 70 cm. Naples MANN 9978

PAGE 176 Fresco showing a cupid. Pompeii, House of Lucretius
Fronto (V,4,a)

CONTENTS

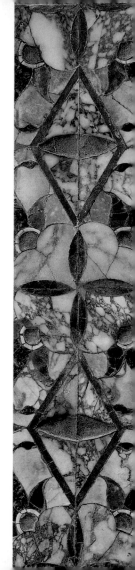

INTRODUCTION

R oman art, more properly Greco-Roman art, reached its peak in the first centuries BC and AD, as Roman power and wealth combined with Greek traditions and workmanship. A treasure trove of the art from this golden age was preserved by terrible chance, when in AD 79 a catastrophic eruption of Mount Vesuvius in southern Italy buried Pompeii and its smaller sister city Herculaneum.

The cities were brought to light again in 1710 with the rediscovery of Herculaneum and its sumptuous Villa of the Papyri, filled with bronze and marble statues. Then in 1748, excavations began at Pompeii, unearthing great public buildings such as the Temple of Isis. These excavations have subsequently revealed approximately two thirds of Pompeii and one third of Herculaneum.

THE CITIES

The population of the cities was a bustling mix. The rich, the poor and slaves were easily spotted through their dress and the wearing (or not) of jewellery – as were foreigners. The majority of the crowd were ordinary citizens, among whom were a large number of freed-men (ex-slaves). Children and women featured greatly in the hubbub. Women, though unable to vote or stand for office, played a major role in society and could possess and dispose of personal wealth, marry and divorce.

The people of the cities watched plays in the theatre, gladiators and beast fights in the amphitheatre, prayed to their gods in the temples, washed and relaxed in the baths and followed court cases and paid their taxes in the Forum. Art was everywhere. Temples, baths and basilicas were decorated with marble, mosaics and painted stucco plaster. Theatres and squares had suites of sculptures depicting benefactors, the imperial family, gods and heroes.

These fine public areas were surrounded by narrow streets lined with shops and houses, two or three storeys high. Streets too had their own art by way of painted signs advertising bars and shops, which showed drinking vessels, animals, birds and gods.

Almost lost in the street were the entrances to homes, from small apartments to luxurious houses. A wealthy home contained a large *familia* (household) with people of all social levels: blood family, slaves, freedmen and tenants. Social mobility was common and many householders had, only years before, been slaves.

ART IN THE HOUSE

Art beautified the house and impressed visitors. Rooms featuring decorative schemes, which linked floors, walls, and ceilings, proclaimed wealth and status. Ceilings of plaster or wood were brightly painted. Simple floors were made of crushed tile and mortar, while finer rooms had floors of *opus sectile* (cut marble shapes) or mosaic (made using small cubes of coloured stone). A central panel or *emblema* was made from very fine cubes and showed detailed subjects, such as still life and scenes from the theatre.

But the star elements of interior design were wall paintings, also called frescoes. Fashions in frescoes changed over time. Styles of the second and first centuries BC created ambitious illusions of architecture and perspective. From around 30 BC frescoes featured blocks of colour (in particular red, yellow and black) with central panels showing scenes from Greek mythology, and smaller panels and motifs depicting landscapes, daily life, still life, animals or people. Some painted walls were completely covered with large-scale scenes of gods, wild animal hunts or gardenscapes, filled with plants and birds. Rarer wall decorations included finely carved marble panels and glass mosaics, which adorned external areas such as garden walls and fountains.

Sculpture, usually on a small scale, featured in particular in the garden or the atrium. Garden sculptures showed animals and deities such as Venus, Hercules and Bacchus with his followers. In the atrium a very Roman form of sculpture was often found – the realistic portrait, a visible display of the family's pedigree and its power.

This lavish décor was the backdrop for daily activities in the household, represented by thousands of objects, from statuettes of gods for household shrines to attractive tableware of silver, pottery and glass. Even functional cooking utensils and containers, fountain spouts and toiletry items were attractive. But some articles were purely decorative. Gold bracelets, armlets, necklaces and rings, set with pearls and emeralds, shone on many of the women of the cities.

These works of art, from jewellery to wall paintings, were commissioned, purchased, used and admired, and therefore we should not view them as artefacts, but rather as possessions of real people who lived, laughed and loved in Pompeii and Herculaneum.

MYTHOLOGY

Images of the gods, as part of domestic and civic worship, or as part of Greek and Roman mythology, were everywhere in the cities.

Worship of the gods was an important part of daily life. It took place at public temples, but also in the home, where domestic shrines (*lararia*) were decorated with paintings and statuettes of the gods. Particularly important were the spirits who protected the household itself, called *lares*. The shrines were usually found in busy areas of the house, especially the atrium, kitchen and garden, and members of the family made offerings at them.

Gods and mythological heroes also featured extensively in the decorative art of the cities, from wall paintings to garden statues, jewellery and drinking cups. Some of the most commonly depicted deities were Venus (the patron of Pompeii), Cupid (Venus' mischievous son) and Bacchus (the wine god), together with his followers, satyrs and maenads. Greek heroes such as Perseus and Theseus, and mythological creatures such as half-man, half-horse centaurs were also very popular. The abundance of such imagery in the home shows the importance of these Greek mythological themes to Roman culture.

14

21

37

ORNAMENT

The wealthy houses in Pompeii and Herculaneum reflected the status of their owners through their decoration. They had floors of mosaic or of expensive cut marble from all over the Roman Empire, ceilings of brightly painted, coffered wood, and painted walls, intricately embellished with scenes of mythology and daily life.

These beautifully adorned rooms provided a suitably impressive setting for displays of family wealth. In the atrium, silverware was displayed on a special table (*cartibulum*) designed to impress visitors to the house. The most valued silver drinking cups featured decoration in high relief, often showing Bacchus, god of wine, and his followers.

It was not just the houses that were ornamented, but the people themselves. Wealthy women had jewellery of the highest quality and craftsmanship – heavy gold bracelets and armlets in the form of beautifully detailed snakes are amongst the finest examples. Rings were set with seal stones of red carnelian or garnet, while earrings, necklaces and body chains were hung with pearls, emeralds and rock crystal.

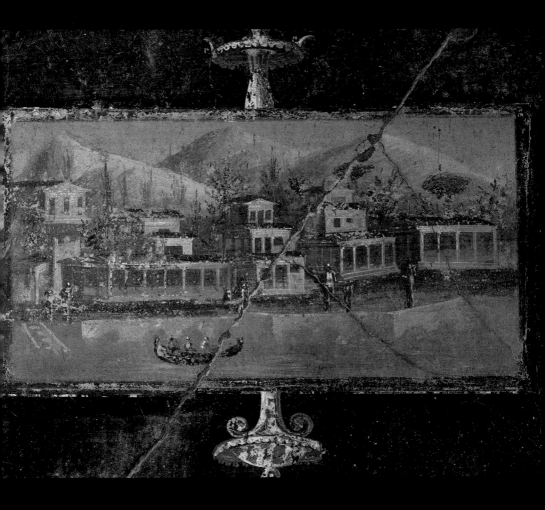

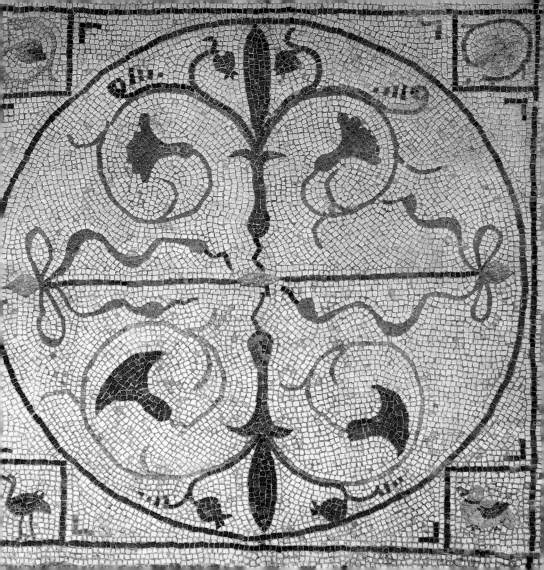

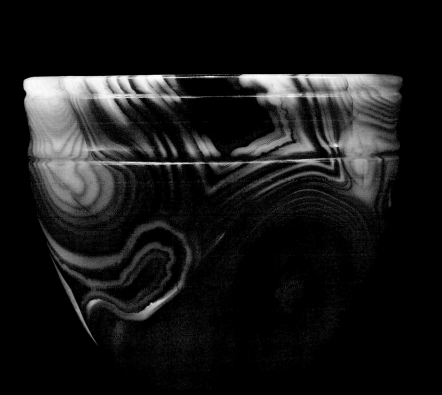

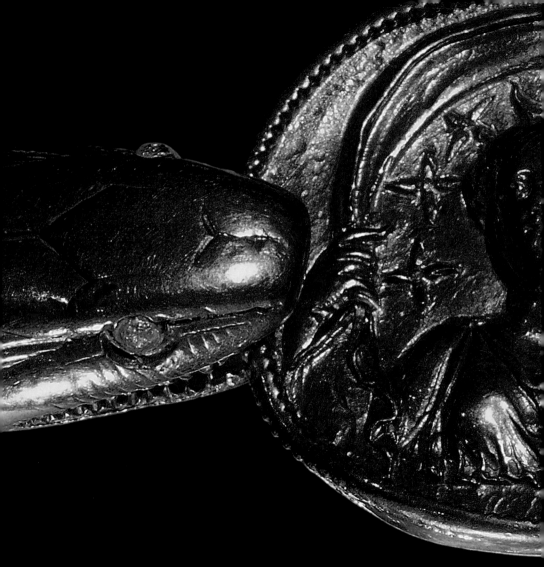

LIVING AND LOVING

Pompeii and Herculaneum preserve a sense of the vibrant lives of their inhabitants in everything from wall paintings, with fascinating scenes of daily life, to the beautifully crafted objects used for routine activities.

Wall paintings show scenes of civic life in the forum – a centre for religion, commerce, administration and business – with its grand equestrian statues and imposing architecture. The business life of the cities can be seen in depictions of products, such as bottles of fish sauce (*garum*), and also in still life paintings of money and implements used in finance and record-keeping.

More commonly depicted in wall paintings were scenes of life within the home. Entertaining guests at dinner and drinking parties was a fundamental part of Roman culture. These parties were often shown in art, in addition to images of the food which was served, including fruit, fish and loaves of bread. Objects such as glass drinking cups and bronze water heaters fulfilled both a functional and decorative role during both parties and everyday meals.

Even the privacy of the bedroom was the subject of wall paintings, with intimate scenes of love-making decorating the walls of some houses.

G·I·F·SCO
SCAVRI
EX·OFFI
NA·SCAV
RI

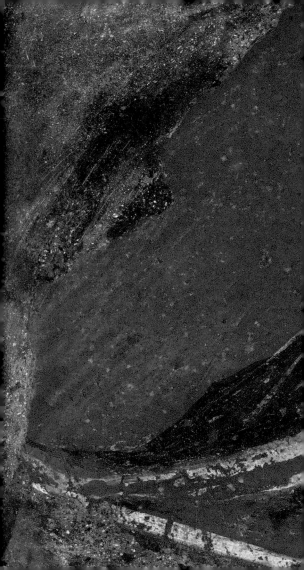

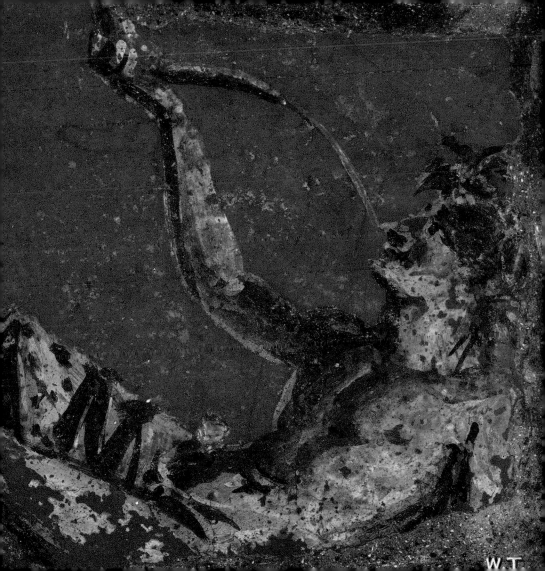

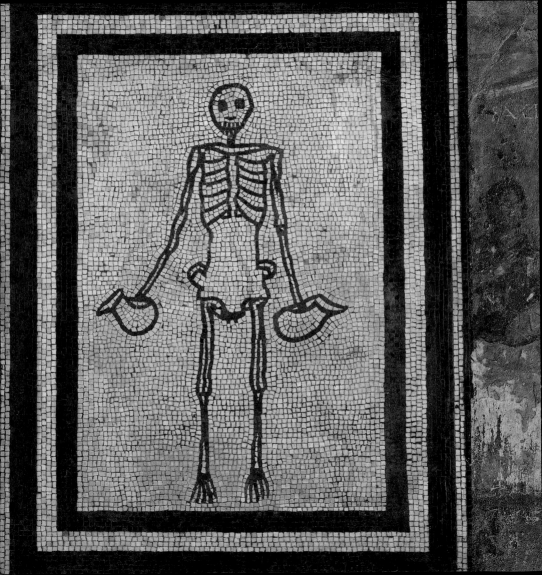

VOBIS·SV...AVITER·EGO·CANTO...ESPITAV...ALE...

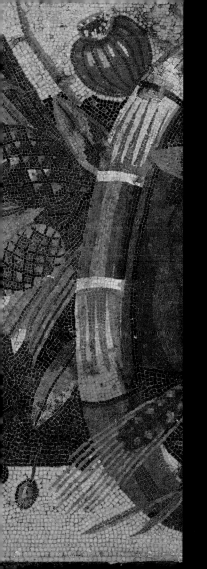

PORTRAITS

Realistic portraits are one of the defining forms of Roman art. Pompeii and Herculaneum have preserved many examples, giving us a good idea of the actual appearance of the people living in the cities.

Public buildings and spaces were adorned with both marble and bronze statues of the emperor and the imperial family, as well as wealthy and influential citizens. Within the home, portraits represented the owner of the house, members of his family or celebrated ancestors. Alongside these marble and bronze portraits were lifelike images captured in wall paintings.

Due to their burial and later discovery, a remarkable number of bronze statues – rare survivals from the Roman world – were preserved. In their original state they would have been highly polished to gleam like gold, sometimes with inlaid copper or silver details. Marble statues often had a more colourful appearance, and some still preserve part of their original painted decoration.

The portraits found in the cities reflected changing fashions, such as hairstyles which were inspired by the imperial portraits produced in Rome. The influence of Greek culture was also very strong in this period; some portraits showed figures from Greek history or mythology, while others sported Greek dress or hairstyles.

NATURE

The Romans were fascinated by the natural world and regularly featured it in their art.

The plants and animals of the wild countryside were brought into the civilized environment of the home through the decoration of walls, floors and furnishings. Reception and dining rooms around the garden were sometimes painted with beautiful scenes of flora and fauna, creating a luxurious setting for entertaining and relaxing, which delighted the family and impressed their guests.

The painted plants and birds are so detailed that they can be identified; visitors could pick out roses and poppies alongside blackbirds, wood pigeons and the more unusual purple swamp hen. The garden itself was a logical setting for natural imagery. Amongst the fountains, benches and flowerbeds were sculptures, mosaics and paintings showing a variety of plants and wildlife.

In addition to familiar animals such as dogs, rabbits and frogs, Roman art depicted more exotic creatures. The panther, sacred to the god Bacchus, and creatures which lived along the River Nile, such as hippopotamuses, were particularly popular. In a way, these animals represented the power of the Roman Empire and the different environments that were under its control.

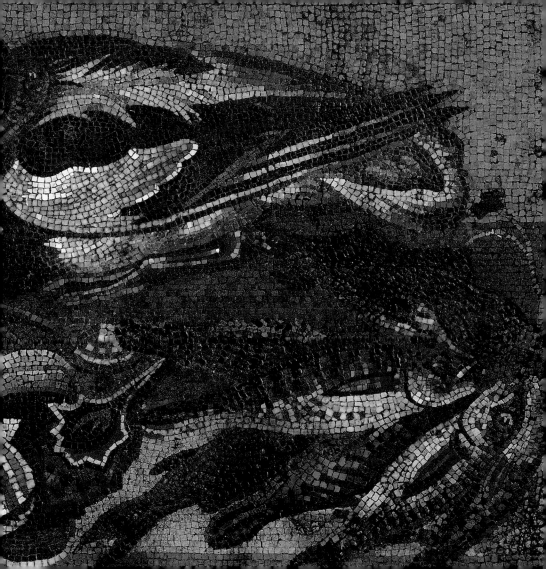

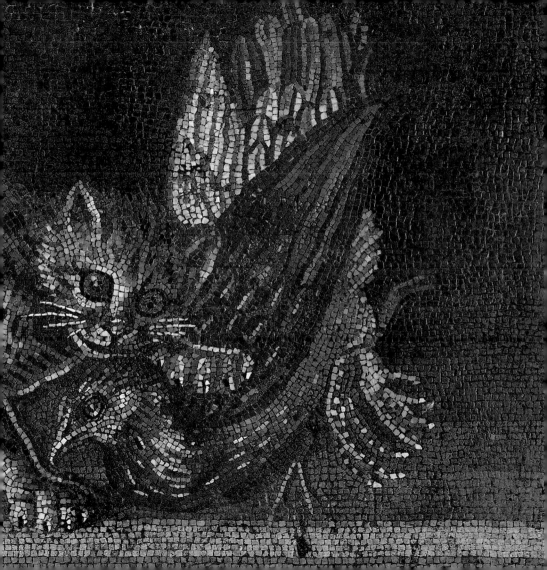

MYTHOLOGY

Shrine (*lararium*) showing Mercury, Bacchus and household gods
Pompeii, Bar of Lucius Vetutius Placidus (I,8,8–9)

Fresco showing cupids and a tripod
Herculaneum, Decumanus Maximus
H. 96 cm, W. 89 cm
Herculaneum, SAP 77872

Fresco showing a cupid
Pompeii, House of Venus in a Shell (II,3,3)

Marble relief showing a satyr and a maenad
Herculaneum, House of the Dionysian Reliefs (Ins.Or.1)
H. 39.5 cm, W. 97 cm
Herculaneum, SAP 79613

Fresco showing Bacchus next to Mount Vesuvius
Pompeii, House of the Centenary (IX,8,3–6)
H. 130 cm, W. 90 cm
Naples, MANN 112286

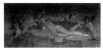

Fresco showing Venus reclining in a shell
Pompeii, House of Venus in a Shell (II,3,3)

Fresco frieze showing centaurs
Pompeii, House of the Menander (I,10,4)

Marble statue of a satyr pouring wine
Herculaneum, House of the Stags (IV,21)
H. 75.2 cm, W. 43.2 cm
Herculaneum, SAP 75797

Marble statue of Pan and the goat
Herculaneum, Villa of the Papyri
H. 44 cm
Naples, MANN 27709

Fresco showing a satyr and a maenad
Pompeii, House of Caecilius Iucundus (V,1,26)
H. 51 cm, W. 52.7 cm
Naples, MANN 110590

Fresco showing a cupid
Pompeii, House of Lucretius Fronto (V,4,a)

Marble decorative disc (*oscillum*)
Pompeii
Diam. 30.5 cm
British Museum, London
1856,1226.1671

Fresco roundel showing Venus
Pompeii, House of Fabius Rufus (VII,16,17–22)

Fresco showing Flora, goddess of flowers and Spring
Stabiae, Villa of Ariadne
H. 39.5 cm, W. 32.5 cm
Naples, MANN 8834

Fresco showing Medea
Stabiae, Villa of Ariadne
H. 38 cm, W. 26 cm
Naples, MANN 8978

Fresco showing Leda and the swan
Stabiae, Villa of Ariadne
H. 44 cm, W. 32 cm
Naples, MANN 9546

Fresco showing the goddess Diana
Stabiae, Villa of Ariadne
H. 37 cm, W. 27 cm
Naples, MANN 9243

Silver statuette of the goddess Fortuna
Pompeii, Porta Nola
H. 3.8 cm, W. 1.5 cm
Pompeii, SAP 15496

Fresco showing Venus and baby cupid
Pompeii, House of Fabius Rufus (VII,16,17–22)

Bronze statuette showing Bacchus riding a panther
Pompeii, House of Pansa (VI,6,1)
H. 20 cm
Naples, MANN 4563

Marble statue of the drunken Hercules
Herculaneum, House of the Stags (IV,21)
H. 55.4 cm, W. 31.5 cm
Herculaneum, SAP 75802

Fresco showing Cassandra clinging to the statue of Athena in Troy
Pompeii, House of the Menander (I,10,4)

Fresco showing Venus
Pompeii, House of Venus in a Shell (II,3,3)

Fresco showing Narcissus
gazing at his reflection
Pompeii, House of Lucretius
Fronto (V,4,a)

Marble relief showing a
ceremony in honour of Bacchus
Herculaneum, House of the
Dionysian Reliefs (Ins.Or.1)
H. 56 cm, W. 109.5 cm
Herculaneum, SAP 88091

Fresco showing Venus
and Mars
Pompeii, House of Fabius
Rufus (VII,16,17–22)

Bronze statuette of a
household god (Lar)
Pompeii (I,11,5)
H. 29 cm
Pompeii, SAP 12840

Fresco showing Theseus
and the Minotaur
Pompeii, House of Gavius
Rufus (VII,2,16)
H. 97 cm, W. 88 cm
Naples, MANN 9043

Fresco showing Perseus
and Andromeda
Pompeii, House of the
Dioscuri (VI,9,6)
H. 128 cm, W. 106 cm
Naples, MANN 8998

Glass wall mosaic showing
Neptune and Amphitrite
Herculaneum, House of
Neptune and Amphitrite
(V,6–7)

Cameo glass plaque with
a Bacchic scene
Pompeii, House of Fabius
Rufus (VII,16,22)
H. 25.5 cm, L. 39.5 cm
Naples, MANN 153651

ORNAMENT

Fresco in the Fourth Style
Pompeii, House of the Prince
of Naples (VI,15,8)

Fresco showing a
woman carrying a tray
Pompeii, Villa of the
Mysteries

Fresco panel showing a
seaside villa
Pompeii, House of Lucretius
Fronto (V,4,a)

Silver drinking cup (scyphus)
decorated with gilded ivy leaves
Pompeii, House of the Silver
Treasure (VI,7,20)
H. 12 cm, Diam. 11 cm
Naples, MANN 25379

Mosaic panel featuring
floral motifs and birds
Pompeii, House of the
Ephebe (I,7,11)

Fresco panel showing fish
Pompeii, House of Lucretius
Fronto (V,4,a)

Fresco showing a table
displaying silverware
Pompeii, Tomb of Gaius
Vestorius Priscus

Silver cup on three feet
in the form of lion heads
Herculaneum
H. 7 cm, Diam. 10.3 cm
Naples, MANN 25601

Gold snake bracelets
Herculaneum, ancient
shoreline, vault IX, skeleton 65
Diam. 9.3 cm
Herculaneum, SAP 78358–9

Painted marble panel showing
women playing knucklebones
Herculaneum, House of
Neptune and Amphitrite (V,6–7)
H. 42 cm, W. 49 cm
Naples, MANN 9562

Floor in cut marble
(opus sectile)
Herculaneum, House of the
Relief of Telephus
(Ins.Or.1,2–3)

Cup made of banded agate
Herculaneum, ancient shoreline,
vault VII, skeleton no. 3
H. 5.5 cm, Diam. 5 cm
Herculaneum, SAP 78969

Gold armlet with two snake
heads holding a disc
Diam. 10.5 cm
Pompeii, House of the Golden
Bracelet (VI,17,42)
Pompeii, SAP 14268

Fresco in the Fourth Style
showing the god Bacchus
Pompeii, House of Julius
Polybius (IX,13,3)

Blue glass lidded vessel (pyxis)
Pompeii (II,1,3)
H. 6.7 cm, Diam. 13 cm
Pompeii, SAP 10232

Floor in cut marble and
glass (opus sectile) with
geometric patterns
Pompeii, House of the
Ephebe (I,7,11)

Polychrome mosaic showing marine life
Pompeii, House of the Menander (I,10,4)

Silver drinking cup (*cantharus*) with cupids
Pompeii, House of Inachus and Io (VI,7,19)
H. 14 cm, Diam. 10 cm
Naples, MANN 25381

Fresco showing a boy reading a scroll
Pompeii, Villa of the Mysteries

Fragment of First Style fresco imitating marble
Pompeii, House of the Fleet (VI,10,11)
H. 50 cm, W. 53 cm
Pompeii, SAP 87283

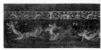

Fresco frieze showing cupids riding chariots
Pompeii, House of the Chaste Lovers (IX,12,6)

Mosaic showing a slave with a large phallus carrying two wine jugs
Pompeii, House of the Menander (I,10,4)

Mosaic panel featuring a Nilotic scene with pygmies
Pompeii, House of the Menander (I,10,4)

Fresco showing a flying couple in a roundel
Pompeii, House of the Chaste Lovers (IX,12,6)

Fresco showing satyrs looking into a bowl
Pompeii, Villa of the Mysteries

Gold ring with snake heads
Oplontis, Villa B, room 10, skeleton no. 27
Diam. 2.4 cm
Naples, MANN 73403

Gold bracelet of paired spheres
Pompeii
L. 9.5 cm
British Museum, London 1946,0702.1

Gold ring with an incised red garnet gem showing birds
Herculaneum, ancient shoreline, vault IX, skeleton 65
Diam. 2 cm
Herculaneum, SAP 78355

Gold bar earrings with pearls
Oplontis, Villa B, room 10, skeleton no. 27
L. (max.) 3.4 cm, W. (max.) 5 cm
Naples, MANN 73407

Fresco showing a seated woman with a mirror
Stabiae, Villa Ariadne
H. 50 cm, W. 33 cm
Naples, MANN 9088

Silver handled mirror
Pompeii, House of Inachus and Io (VI,7,19)
H. 30.5 cm, Diam. (face) 18 cm
Naples, MANN 25718

Fresco in the Third Style
Pompeii, House of Lucretius Fronto (V,4,a)

A selection of jewellery found with a woman
Oplontis, Villa B, room 10, skeleton no. 27
Naples, MANN 73410; 73412a; 73409; 73401; 73412b–c; 73408; 73404; 73403

Silver bowl with fluted edges
Pompeii, House of Inachus and Io (VI,7,19)
H. 5.5 cm, Diam. 12 cm
Naples, MANN 25554

Fresco showing initiation rites
Pompeii, Villa of the Mysteries

LIVING AND LOVING

Fresco showing a drinking party
Pompeii, House of the Chaste Lovers (IX,12,6–7)

Mosaic showing a guard dog with the message 'Beware of the dog' (*CAVE CANEM*)
Pompeii, House of the Tragic Poet (VI,8,3–5)

Pottery cup decorated with a face
Herculaneum, House of the Gem (Ins.Or.1)
H. 9.2 cm, Diam. 13.5 cm
Herculaneum, SAP 76550

Shrine (*lararium*) painted on a kitchen wall
Terzigno, villa 6
H. 223 cm, W. 286.5 cm
Pompeii, SAP 86755

Bronze wind-chime
(*tintinnabulum*) with a
hanging lamp
Pompeii
H. 21 cm, W. 18 cm
Pompeii, SAP 1260

Panel from a fresco showing
coins and writing implements
Pompeii, Praedia of Julia Felix
(II,4,3–12)
H. 298 cm, W. 447 cm
Naples, MANN 8598

Fresco showing a man
with a drinking horn (*rhyton*)
Pompeii
H. 14.5 cm, W. 21.5 cm
British Museum, London
1856,1226.1623

Marble relief showing
Pompeii during an earthquake
Pompeii, House of Caecilius
Iucundus (V,1,26)
H. 13.5, L. 87.5
Naples, MANN 20470

Green glass handled cup
(*modiolus*)
Pompeii, House of the
Menander (I,10,4)
H. 12 cm, Diam. 13 cm
Pompeii, SAP 4960

Fresco showing a drinking
party
Pompeii, House of the
Chaste Lovers (IX,12,6–7)

Fresco showing a group
of men reading a notice set
up in the forum
Pompeii, Praedia of Julia Felix
(II,4,3)
H. 64 cm, W. 48 cm

Fresco depicting the
distribution of bread
Pompeii (VII,3,30)
H. 69 cm, W. 60 cm
Naples, MANN 9071

Fresco showing a panel
with fish
Pompeii, House of the Chaste
Lovers (IX,12,6–7)

Fresco showing a bowl of dates
and dried figs with a glass of wine
Herculaneum, House of the
Stags (IV,21)
H. 40 cm, W. 119 cm
Naples, MANN 8645

Fresco showing a loaf of
bread and two figs
Herculaneum, House
of the Stags (IV,21)
H. 23 cm, W. 23 cm
Naples, MANN 8625

Bronze vessel for heating
water (*samovar*)
Pompeii
H. 41 cm, Diam. 27 cm
Naples, MANN 111048

Bronze ornament In the
shape of a female head
Herculaneum, Decumanus
Maximus
H. 14 cm, W. 6.5 cm
Herculaneum, SAP 77838

Mosaic showing a skeleton
holding two wine jugs (*askoi*)
Pompeii (VI,Ins.Occ.19–26)
H. 91 cm, W. 70 cm
Naples, MANN 9978

Fresco showing a dinner
party with a singing guest
Pompeii, House of the
Triclinium (V,2,4)
H. 60 cm, W. 64 cm
Naples, MANN 120031

Fresco showing a private
dining scene
Herculaneum
H. 66 cm, W. 66 cm
Naples, MANN 9024

Fresco showing a music
lesson
Pompeii
H. 58 cm, W. 80 cm
British Museum, London
1867,0508.1353

Fresco showing a man
and woman making love
Pompeii, House of the
Centenary (IX,8,3–6)

Mosaic panel showing
a theatrical mask
Pompeii, House of Fabius
Rufus (VII,16,17–22)

Pottery bottle for fish sauce
(*garum*) with painted
inscription (*dipinto*)
Pompeii
H. 24 cm
Pompeii, SAP 81744

Mosaic showing a *garum*
bottle with an inscription
Pompeii, House of Umbricius
Scaurus (VII,16,15)
H. 74 cm, W. 31 cm
Pompeii, SAP 15190

Mosaic showing a theatrical
mask and garlands
Pompeii, House of the Faun
(VI,12,2)
H. 49 cm, W. 280 cm
Naples, MANN 9994

Terracotta statuette
of a mother and child
Herculaneum, Cardo V drain

Fresco showing a dinner party
Pompeii, House of the
Triclinium (V,2,4)
H. 68 cm, W. 66 cm
Naples, MANN 120029

Fresco showing a man
and woman making love
Pompeii, House of Caecilius
Iucundus (V,1,26)
H. 51.7 cm, W. 44 cm
Naples, MANN 110569

PORTRAITS

Marble statue of a young boy
Herculaneum, Villa of the Papyri
H. 129 cm
Naples, MANN 6105

Mosaic portrait of a woman
Pompeii (VI,15,14)
H. 34 cm, W. 29 cm
Naples, MANN 124666

Marble portrait of the Hellenistic ruler Pyrrhus
Herculaneum, Villa of the Papyri
H. 46 cm
Naples, MANN 6150

Fresco showing a young man with a scroll labelled 'Homer'
Pompeii, House of the Apartment (V,2,h)
H. 44.4 cm, W. 44.8 cm
Naples, MANN 120620a

Fresco showing a young man with a scroll labelled 'Plato'
Pompeii, House of the Apartment (V,2,h)
H. 44.8 cm, W. 44.7 cm
Naples, MANN 12062b

Bronze portrait of a man
Pompeii, House of the Citharist (I,4,5)
H. 37.5 cm, W. 23.5 cm
Naples, MANN 4989

Marble portrait of a woman
Herculaneum
H. 50 cm, W. 19.5 cm
Naples, MANN 6247

Fresco showing a woman's face
Herculaneum
H. 19.7 cm, W. 15.4 cm
Naples, MANN 9094

Bronze statue of Lucius Mammius Maximus
Herculaneum, Theatre
H. 227 cm, W. 105 cm
Naples, MANN 5591

Bronze statue showing a woman fastening her dress (so-called *danzatrice*)
Herculaneum, Villa of the Papyri
H. 150 cm
Naples, MANN 5619

Bronze statue of a woman (so-called *danzatrice*)
Herculaneum, Villa of the Papyri
H. 153 cm
Naples, MANN 5620

Bronze statue of a woman (so-called *danzatrice*)
Herculaneum, Villa of the Papyri
H. 151 cm
Naples, MANN 5605

Bronze statue of a woman (so-called *danżatrice*)
Herculaneum, Villa of the Papyri
H. 150 cm
Naples, MANN 5604

Bronze statue of a woman (so-called *danzatrice*)
Herculaneum, Villa of the Papyri
H. 155 cm
Naples, MANN 5621

Fresco showing the baker Terentius Neo and his wife
Pompeii, House of Terentius Neo (VII,2,6)
H. 60 cm, W. 70 cm
Naples, MANN 9058

Gold coin (*aureus*) of the emperor Nero
Herculaneum
Herculaneum, SAP 78394

Wooden female portrait, perhaps of an ancestor
Herculaneum, House of the Wattlework (III,13–15)
H. 30.4 cm, Diam. 12.5 cm
Herculaneum, SAP 75598

Bronze and marble herm of Lucius Caecilius Iucundus
Pompeii, House of Lucius Caecilius Iucundus (V,1,26)
H. 173 cm, W. 35 cm
Naples, MANN 110663

Marble statue of the priestess Eumachia
Pompeii, Building of Eumachia
H. 194 cm
Naples, MANN 6232

Fresco showing a man and a woman
Pompeii
Diam. 14 cm
British Museum, London 1856,1226.1621

Fresco roundel with the portrait of a young woman
Pompeii, House of the Gilded Cupids (VI,16,7)

Fresco showing a woman holding writing implements (so-called *Sappho*)
Pompeii (VI,Ins.Occ.)
H. 37 cm, W. 38 cm
Naples, MANN 9084

Bronze statue of the empress Livia
Herculaneum, Theatre
H. 214 cm, W. 100 cm
Naples, MANN 5589

Fresco roundel with the portrait of a little girl
Pompeii, House of Lucretius Fronto (V,4,a)

Fresco roundel with the
portrait of a boy dressed
as Mercury
Pompeii, House of Lucretius
Fronto (V,4,a)

NATURE

Fresco showing garden scene
Pompeii, House of the
Golden Bracelet (VI,17,42)
H. 400 cm, W. 370 cm
Pompeii, SAP 40690

Detail from a fresco garden
scene showing a jay
Pompeii, House of the
Golden Bracelet (VI,17,42)
Pompeii, SAP 40691

Detail from a fresco garden
scene showing a blackbird
Pompeii, House of the
Golden Bracelet (VI,17,42)
Pompeii, SAP 40691

Detail from a fresco garden
scene showing a golden
oriole
Pompeii, House of the
Golden Bracelet (VI,17,42)
Pompeii, SAP 40691

Fresco showing a bird
eating figs
Oplontis, Villa B

Detail from a fresco garden
scene showing a wood
pigeon by a fountain
Pompeii, House of the
Golden Bracelet (VI,17,42)
Pompeii, SAP 40690

Detail from a fresco garden
scene showing a nightingale
perched on a stake
Pompeii, House of the
Golden Bracelet (VI,17,42)
Pompeii, SAP 40692

Detail from a
fresco garden scene
Pompeii, House of the
Golden Bracelet (VI,17,42)
Pompeii, SAP 40692

Faience fountain spout
in the form of a frog
Pompeii
H. 17.5 cm, W. 23 cm
Naples, MANN 121322

Detail from a fresco garden
scene showing a purple
swamp hen
Pompeii, House of the
Golden Bracelet (VI,17,42)
Pompeii, SAP 40690

Fresco showing a
bird drinking from
an ornate bird bath
Oplontis, Villa B

Marble table with
support (monopodium)
in the form of a panther
Pompeii (V,4c)
H. 89 cm
Pompeii, SAP 54947

Mosaic showing sea
creatures
Pompeii (VIII,2,16)
H. 103 cm, W. 103 cm
Naples, MANN 120177

Mosaic showing a Nilotic
scene
Pompeii, House of the Faun
(VI,12,2)
H. 70 cm, W. 333 cm
Naples, MANN 9990

Mosaic showing a dog
Pompeii, House of Orpheus
(VI,14,20)
H. 80 cm, W. 80 cm
Naples, MANN 110666

Fresco showing a peacock
Oplontis, Villa B

Fresco showing a rabbit
and some figs
Pompeii
H. 35 cm, W. 42 cm
Naples, MANN 8630

Bronze fountain spout
in the form of a peacock
Pompeii, House of Camillus
(VII,12,22–24)
H. 30 cm, W. 11.5 cm
Naples, MANN 69784

Marble statue of a stag
and hounds
Herculaneum, House of the
Stags (IV,21)
H. 63.7 cm, W. 62.7 cm
Herculaneum, SAP 75796

Marble statue of a stag
and hounds
Herculaneum, House of the
Stags (IV,21)
H. 67.5 cm, W. 62.7 cm
Herculaneum, SAP 75801

Upper section of a mosaic
showing a cat and a bird
Pompeii, House of the Faun
(VI,12,2)
H. 51 cm, W. 51 cm
Naples, MANN 9993

Lower section of a mosaic showing
ducks, birds, fish and shells
Pompeii, House of the Faun
(VI,12,2)
H. 51 cm, W. 51 cm
Naples, MANN 9993

Further information
about the British
Museum and its
collection can be
found on the website
at britishmuseum.org